AF481161

Ju Bear:

I Am Four

Celebrating you, my precious son
Always in my heart, forever near.

1
ONE

I could barely crawl,

I would smile and giggle at every little thing,

When I was Two

And chew on toys and books brand new.

And explore the world
with my curious feet.

3
THREE

The world was new,

I loved to run, jump, skip and hop,

Now I am four

Asking questions of everyone I see.

From counting numbers
to bouncing a ball.

Monday
Tuesday
Wednesday
Thursday
Friday
Saturday
Sunday

And let my curiosity lead the way.

I will keep on spreading my wings.